W9-BTP-084

Arnulfo L. Oliveira Memorial Library

UTB
TSC

CONNECTICUT

The Spirit of America

Text by Patricia Harris and David Lyon

Harry N. Abrams, Inc., Publishers

NEW YORK

This series was originated by Walking Stick Press, San Francisco
Series Designer: Linda Herman; Series Editor: Diana Landau

For Harry N. Abrams, Inc.:
   Editor: Nicole Columbus
   Designer: Ana Rogers

Photo research:
   Laurie Platt Winfrey, Leslie Van Lindt, Van Bucher
   Carousel Research, Inc.

Page 1: *Jones Inn* by George Henry Durrie, c. 1855. *Photo Christie's Images*
Page 2: A detail from *Arts of the City,* one of five murals by Thomas Hart Benton
in a 1930s series entitled *The Arts of Life in America.* © *T. H. Benton and R.P. Benton*
Testamentary Trusts/Licensed by VAGA, *New York, N.Y. New Britain Museum of*
American Art

Library of Congress Cataloguing-in-Publication Data
Harris, Patricia, 1949–
   Connecticut : the spirit of America / text by Patricia Harris and David Lyon.
   p.   cm.
   ISBN 0–8109–5568–7
   1. Connecticut—Civilization—Pictorial works.   2. Connecticut—Miscellanea.
   I. Lyon, David, 1949—II. Title.
F95.H37   2000
974.6—dc21   00–035570

Harry N. Abrams, Inc.
100 Fifth Avenue
New York, N.Y. 10011
www.abramsbooks.com

Heart and Hand Valentine, c. 1840–60. Collection of the Museum of American Folk Art, N.Y.

Connecticut Barns in Landscape by **Charles Sheeler, 1934.** *National Museum of American Art, Washington, D.C./Art Resource, N.Y.*

It should be no surprise that Samuel Clemens became an adopted Connecticut Yankee, given his fascination with gadgetry and machines. Holder of three patents of his own, Clemens felt right at home in the state that held more patents per capita than any other in his day and whose early representative, Benjamin Huntington, had first drafted legislation to establish the Patent Office in 1790.

From the outset, Connecticut has been a fount of invention. Its hillsides yielded the first metal ores mined in the British colonies, and its craftsmen were smelting, casting, rolling, and fashioning metal when other colonials were still whittling their necessities from green lumber. Edward and William Pattison fashioned North America's first tinware in 1740 and developed a sys-

> *"If there wasn't any new-fangled quick way to make a thing, I could invent one, and do it as easily as rolling off a log."*
>
> Mark Twain, A Connecticut Yankee in King Arthur's Court, 1899

tem of itinerant peddlers to sell their wares. Eli Whitney revolutionized cotton processing with his gin and went on to create the first assembly lines using interchangeable parts. Phineas Pratt developed the ivory saw to turn out America's first ivory combs, switching later to piano keys. A litany of Connecticut inventions made the state king of commerce in everything from packaged garden seeds and steel fishhooks to derby hats.

Hand in hand with invention and commerce went a profound respect for rules and regulations. Connecticut founded the nation's first law school in 1784; the state had already won greater freedom from royal meddling than its colonial neighbors and had established a system for granting exclusive exploitation rights —such as the first offshore whaling concession, in 1640. Early on, too, it became a leader in the insurance business, an earthbound career that would sustain two great creative artists: composer Charles Ives and poet Wallace Stevens. Connecticut's Yankee peddlers tramped

This humorous yarn reel is made of carved, turned, and polychromed wood, c. 1825–50. *Collection of the Museum of American Folk Art, N.Y.*

the face of an expanding America in ever-widening circles. No wonder the state's distinguished adopted playwrights cast the human lot in a salesman's frame: Eugene O'Neill in *The Iceman Cometh* and Arthur Miller in *Death of a Salesman*.

The theatrical capital of New York lies only 12 miles from the Connecticut border. New Haven's record of exemplary American theater is due partly to this proximity: if the play's a hit, it soon finds a new home on Broadway. New Haven is more than a stopover, though. Yale University's School of Drama produces a steady stream of leading actors, directors, and other stage and screen professionals.

Although Connecticut built its reputation on manufacturing, it retains large stretches of countryside. Its eastern plateau remains as bucolic as in colonial days, and the forested western hills are rich and green. Since the 1970s, the Connecticut River, greatest of the New England waterways, has been restored to nearly pristine condition, with spawning fish and bird life.

Sprinkled throughout this landscape—especially along Long Island Sound and in the Litchfield Hills—are well-kept small towns that shelter performers and artists seeking the genteel charms of the Connecticut countryside. Paul Newman and Joanne Woodward have long made their home here. Writers as diverse as Philip Roth, Arthur Miller, and Frank McCourt have found congenial surroundings in rural Connecticut. But no one quite epitomizes the country squire life like Martha Stewart, who has made Connecticut chic a national style.

Connecticut's artistic traditions run deep. The first art gallery in the U.S. opened at Yale in 1832, and America's first public art museum, the Wadsworth Atheneum in Hartford, a decade later. While the Yale Center for British Art houses the most extensive collection of British art outside England, the New

Pequot Beach, New London, Connecticut by **Nelson Holbrook White, 1994.** *Private collection*

Britain Museum of American Art is the oldest and one of the most complete museums devoted to American art. Nor is Connecticut stuck in the past. The Aldrich Museum of Contemporary Art in Ridgefield, established in 1964, was the first U.S. museum to feature contemporary art exclusively.

Young artists used to leave Connecticut for careers in New York and Boston, but the trend reversed in the 20th century. Arthur Dove spent several years early in his career on a houseboat anchored in Long Island Sound. Alexander Calder set up his studio in tiny Roxbury, attracting a circle of experimental artists. The quintessential New York painter, Robert Motherwell, spent his last quarter century working in Greenwich, bringing an abstract vision to the gentle, diffuse light that so inspired the American Impressionists. Today, with the resurgence of representational painting, the Connecticut shore is lined with easels on a fine summer's day. 🍁

CONNECTICUT

"Constitution State"
(unofficially, "Nutmeg State")
5th State

Date of Statehood
JANUARY 9, 1788

Capital
HARTFORD

Bird
AMERICAN ROBIN

Flower
MOUNTAIN LAUREL

Tree
WHITE OAK (*QUERCUS ALBA*)

Mineral
GARNET

Animal
SPERM WHALE

Shellfish
EASTERN OYSTER

Connecticut officially calls itself the "Constitution State," contending that the state's Fundamental Orders of 1639 were history's first written constitu-

Robin and mountain laurel

tion. Its homelier informal nickname, "Nutmeg State," comes from a tale that early traders sold wooden nutmegs as the genuine item. (Most likely they were whittled by sailors inbound from the Spice Islands and sold as souvenirs.) The origins of the state motto are hazy; it first appeared on the seal of the Saybrook Colony in 1635, linked with the depiction of grapevines. Some believe it derives from Psalm 80: "Thou has brought a vine out of Egypt. . . . " Today's seal preserves three grapevines—and, indeed, Connecticut has a small but flourishing wine industry. The state's symbolic flora are indigenous and evocative: the white oak is honored for the role of the Charter Oak in history, the

"Qui Transtulit Sustinet"
(He Who Transplanted Still Sustains)

State motto, adapted from the Book of Psalms with reference to a vineyard depicted on the colonial seal

lovely mountain laurel because it swathes the hills in pink and white in late spring. The Eastern oyster, a staple of Long Island Sound native tribes, was the basis of an important local industry. And the sperm whale was designated the state animal in 1975 to highlight both its role in Connecticut's past economy and its now endangered status. 🍃

"Yankee Doodle"

Yankee Doodle went to town,
Riding on a pony,
Stuck a feather in his hat,
And called it macaroni.

Yankee Doodle keep it up,
Yankee Doodle dandy,
Mind the music and the step,
And with the folks be handy.

Connecticut's state song, from a folk tune with words by Dr. Shuckburgh (see story, page 15)

Mountain laurel (*Kalmia latifolia*).
Photo Angelina Lax/Photo Researchers
Above: The Connecticut state capitol in Hartford. *Photo Jack McConnell*

Clamburger Special

1 pint clams, finely chopped
1 cup cracker crumbs
1 egg, well beaten
½ tsp. dried parsley
½ tsp. salt
¼ tsp. ground black pepper
2 tbsp. oil

In a medium bowl, mix clams, cracker crumbs, egg, parsley, salt and pepper. Refrigerate 30 minutes. Form mixture into 3-in. round cakes. Heat oil in a large skillet and fry cakes for 2 minutes per side, or until crisp. Drain on paper towels. Serve on toasted rolls with sliced tomatoes, lettuce, and tartar sauce.

Adapted from Mystic Seaport's Seafood Secrets Cookbook

Nathan Hale, State Hero

Born in Coventry in 1755 and educated at Yale, young New London schoolmaster Nathan Hale was commissioned as a lieutenant in the Continental Army in 1775 and soon rose to captain. In response to General Washington's call for a volunteer, he sailed from Norwalk to Long Island in September 1776 and crossed enemy lines to gather information on the British strength and plans. Caught trying to return to his unit, he was hanged without a trial as a spy on September 22, 1776. His final stirring words—paraphrasing a speech in Joseph Addison's stage tragedy *Cato*—stand as a model of patriotism and courage: "I only regret that I have but one life to lose for my country."

Last Words of Captain Nathan Hale, the Hero-Martyr of the American Revolution. **Drawn by F. C. Darley, engraved by A. H. Ritchie.** *Culver Pictures*

Strong as an Oak

The Charter Oak may be the most colorful symbol of Connecticut's love of freedom. In 1687, Sir Edmund Andros arrived in Hartford as an emissary of King James II, demanding the return of Connecticut's hard-won charter of 1660. Negotiations went on into the night, until suddenly patriots snuffed the candles and literally stole the document off the table, squirreling it away in the hollow of an oak tree ever after celebrated as the Charter Oak. The tree survived until a storm toppled it in 1856, but a scion of the original continues to flourish in Bushnell Park within sight of the state capitol.

The Yankee Is Born

When the ragtag colonial troops marched out from Norwalk in 1756, tradition has it that the sister of Colonel Thomas Fitch outfitted all the men with feathers for their hats, saying "Soldiers should wear plumes." Arriving at Fort Crailo to fight the French and Indians, the country boys were subjected to derision, inspiring a British Army surgeon, Dr. Shuckburgh, to exclaim, "Stab my victuals, they're macaronis!"—slang for a fop or dandy. On the spot he composed "Yankee Doodle" to the folk tune of "Lucy Locket Lost Her Pocket." Colonials embraced the jibe, and the tune became a fife-and-drum march standard during the American Revolution.

The Charter Oak, symbol of Connecticut liberty, was represented on the tricentennial commemorative coin. *Photo Jack McConnell.* *Above left:* Antique postcard with Connecticut state seal. *Culver Pictures*

1614   Dutch explorer Adriaen Block sails up the Connecticut River.

1634   Wethersfield, Windsor, and Hartford are settled by the English.

1656   Bequest establishes the nation's first municipal public library in New Haven.

1687   Colonists retain their Charter by hiding it in an oak tree.

1701   Collegiate School founded; moved to New Haven in 1717 and renamed Yale.

1727   Samuel Higley of Simsbury mints the first copper coins in America. They are marked, "I am good copper. Value me as you will."

1740   Edward and William Pattison begin manufacturing tinware in Berlin.

1764   *Connecticut Courant* (now the *Hartford Courant*), oldest continuously published newspaper in America, launched in Hartford by Thomas Green.

1777–81   Danbury, New Haven, Fairfield, and Norwalk raided by British troops; traitor Benedict Arnold attacks New London and Groton.

1783   Protestant Episcopal Church in the U.S. is established after a meeting by Anglican clergy at the Glebe House in Woodbury.

1784   First law school in the U.S. founded in Litchfield.

1788   New England's first woolen mill established in Hartford.

1788   Connecticut becomes the fifth state.

1793–96   Hartford's Old State House, designed by Charles Bulfinch, is built.

1795   First insurance company, Mutual Assurance Company of the City of Norwich, organized.

1796   America's first cookbook, written by Amelia Simmons, is published in Hartford.

1801   "Long nines," the first American cigars, are made in South Windsor.

1814   Hartford Convention strengthens Federalism when, by narrow vote, New England stays in Union.

1815   First steamboat voyage up the Connecticut River to Hartford.

1817   School for the deaf founded in Hartford by Thomas Gallaudet.

1830   The New England Association of Farmers, Mechanics and Other Workingmen becomes the country's first industrial union.

1832   Yale University Art Gallery is the first U.S. art gallery opened to the public.

1835 America's first music school, Music Vale Seminary, founded in Salem.

1839 Africans mutiny on the slave ship *Amistad*, which is captured and towed to New London; the Africans are jailed and tried in New Haven.

1840s–50s Peak period of whaling from Connecticut ports, especially New London.

1842 Wadsworth Atheneum, nation's first public art museum, established in Hartford.

1848 First trains run between New York and New Haven.

1861 Yale University awards the first Ph.D. degree, in philosophy, in the U.S.

1877 First telephone exchange in the world established in New Haven.

1879 New capitol building in Hartford, designed by Richard Upjohn, completed.

1900 Electric Boat in Groton builds the first U.S. Navy submarine, the *Holland*.

1910 U.S. Coast Guard Academy moves to New London.

1929 Marine Historical Association forms in Mystic; name changes to Mystic Seaport in 1978.

1932 Lyman Allyn Museum opens in New London with focus on Connecticut painting and decorative arts.

1938 First section of Merritt Parkway opens.

1939 WDRC-FM, first FM station in the country, begins broadcasting.

1954 First atomic-powered submarine, USS *Nautilus*, is launched in Groton.

1958 Connecticut Turnpike opens.

1974 Ella Grasso is elected governor.

1977 Yale Center for British Art opens in building designed by Louis I. Kahn.

1981 Whitney Museum of American Art opens Stamford branch at Champion International Corporation.

1994 University of Connecticut women's basketball team clinches first of two consecutive national titles.

1998 Connecticut River designated an American Heritage River by President Clinton.

1999 UConn men's basketball team clinches NCAA national title.

1999 Bushnell Memorial Auditorium in Hartford launches major renovation project to create a new theater, scheduled to open in 2001.

2000 Replica of slave ship *Amistad* launched at Mystic Seaport boatyard.

One of its many tributaries joins the Connecticut River south of Hamburg Cove near Essex. *Photo Jack McConnell. Below:* With its deep harbor, Essex excelled at building seagoing vessels for the Caribbean trade in the early 19th century. This ship's figurehead of a lady with a rose dates c. 1800–10. *Courtesy the Mariners' Museum, Newport News, Va.*

Deep River

When the Pleistocene ice sheet withdrew its grip 10,000 years ago, it left a mighty arterial river in the rift valley that bisects New England. The Connecticut River ranges 406 miles from the Canadian border to Long Island Sound, touching five of the six New England states but giving its name only to one. *Connecticut* is the English rendering of an Algonquian name

meaning "at the long tidal river"; Native Americans fished for migratory shad and salmon and farmed the river's floodplain islands and peninsulas.

In the early days of European settlement, the river was a highway for fur pelts from the northern forest. Soon the falls that impeded navigation were harnessed to power machinery, opening the way for industrialization. The Connecticut River remained a conduit for manufactured goods until rail and road rendered barges obsolete in the 20th century. The river's mouth lacked a deep harbor, so the tidal marshes and estuaries of the lower reaches escaped extensive development. Even today, the subtle grasses and reeds that so attracted the American Impressionist painters continue to harbor waterfowl and richly diverse wildlife. The Nature Conservancy has designated the lower Connecticut River as one of a handful of the world's "Last Great Places."

The First Wildlife

Some 200 million years ago the swampy plains around what is now Rocky Hill ran amuck with some of the first large flesh-eating dinosaurs, *Eubrontes*. Members of the Ceratosaur group, they averaged 8 feet tall and 18 feet long. More than 2,000 tracks—but no bones—were discovered by bulldozer operators in 1966, one of the largest concentrations of dinosaur tracks ever found in a single geological layer in North America. About 500 tracks—the official state fossil—are preserved under a geodesic dome at Dinosaur State Park.

Fall foliage. *Photo Jack McConnell*

Exaltation of the Hills

The low, eroded hills of western Connecticut begin in the north as rugged bedrock with dramatic, glacier-cut ravines where cold mountain streams rush through the clefts. Proceeding south toward Long Island Sound, the peaks and valleys moderate into the genteel and rolling Litchfield Hills, where ancient hay meadows have returned to hardwood forest, and rambling colonial-era farms have often been converted to artfully landscaped summer estates. The only New England mountains extensively settled before the Revolution, the western hill towns look like quintessential colonial-era New England: broad commons, white clapboard houses, and high-spired white churches.

Quiet Corner

The undulating uplands of northeastern Connecticut are little altered since 17th-century settlement. With its broad fields demarcated by lichen-crusted stone walls and tiny towns built around mill falls, the Quiet Corner clings to a bucolic past. The valley of the Quinebaug and Shetucket Rivers is a National Heritage Corridor, the "last green valley" between Washington and Boston. Even major roads traverse a landscape where horse traffic would seem more natural than autos. Splendidly pastoral in one of America's most industrialized states, the Quiet Corner was recognized by the federal Department of Transportation in designating Route 169 as one of its first scenic byways.

Drifting Snow, Grandview Farm by Peter Poskas, 1999. The Connecticut farmhouse was the original modular home, accreting block additions to the basic colonial box, making an L-turn here and there to present a wide face to the southerly sun. *Courtesy Schmidt Bingham Gallery*

Beach Scene, New London by William J. Glackens, 1918. A member of The Eight, a turn-of-the-century group of realist painters who organized around Robert Henri, Glackens later became absorbed by Impressionism, modeling his style after Renoir. *Columbus Museum of Art, Ohio*

Long Island Soundings

Daniel Webster dubbed Long Island Sound "the Mediterranean of the western hemisphere." Shielded from the brunt of the Atlantic Ocean by New York's Long Island, Connecticut's 253-mile shore shows a homogeneity rare in New England. Long stretches of sandy beach separate tidal marshes at the mouths of rivers draining the interior highlands. Only the Thames River offers good deepwater anchorages, where New London and Groton developed as major ports. But the ingenuity of boatbuilders in nearby Stonington and Mystic created a substantial inshore fishing fleet, often pulling nets and lines with small, maneuverable sail craft. The southern shore near New York soon developed as a manufacturing district, using

In the late 19th and early 20th centuries, the beaches of the Sound became summer playgrounds served from New York by railroads.
Photo Jack McConnell

shallow-draft coasting schooners to send goods to market. Among the first to ride the rails from Manhattan were the plein-air American Impressionist painters, who found their own Giverny in the coastal villages of southern Connecticut.

Sea Dog of the Sound

The green-capped archipelago of about 100 Thimble Islands (named for their thimble-shaped blackberries) at mid-coast proved irresistible to pirate Captain Kidd, since they were the perfect base to plunder vessels passing through Long Island Sound. Treasure hunters still search for the pirate's cache, by legend hidden in a Money Island cave with an underwater entrance.

Dioramas at the
Mashantucket Pequot
Museum and Research
Center attempt to
reconstruct Pequot
living patterns before
European contact.
Photo Jack McConnell

First Peoples of Connecticut

Prior to European contact, the land now known as Connecticut was thinly populated by four Algonquian-speaking Native American groups, of which the best organized were the bellicose Pequots and their close relatives (and political enemies) the Mohegans. Intermittent warfare in the previous century had left the Pequots in control of the area east of the Connecticut River, and they had subjugated most of the river tribes. When white settlement began, conflict was inevitable; in the Pequot War of 1637, combined English and Mohegan forces virtually eradicated the Pequots in a bloody last stand at Mystic. The Mohegans, who fought with the English in King Philip's War of 1675–76, were decimated by European diseases by 1700, and total tribal rolls in Connecticut shrank to about 160 by the 1930s.

That population figure still holds, but after successful suits to win federal tribal recognition in the 1970s, both the Pequots and the Mohegans have vastly improved their economic lots by operating some of the world's most profitable gambling casinos on tribal land. The Mashantucket Pequot Museum & Research Center, funded by casino profits, attempts to reconstruct precontact Pequot village life and holds historical and genealogical records of the tribe.

The Pequot War destroyed the tribe's dominance of central and eastern Connecticut and nearly exterminated the Pequot people. *Library of Congress*

Guilford's Congregational Church, constructed in 1829, epitomizes the full-blown development of the Greek Revival style in New England public architecture. *Connecticut Historical Society Right:* In the 1630s, English settlers squabbled with the Dutch, who had established a trading post at Hartford. Ultimately the Dutch withdrew from the Connecticut River Valley. *Corbis-Bettmann*

Furs and farmland drew the first Europeans to the Connecticut River Valley. In 1614 the great Dutch navigator, Adriaen Block, found his way around the shoals off Saybrook and Lyme and sailed up the Connecticut River as far as Enfield. He reported canoes laden with furs from the northern forest, and for the next 18 years New Amsterdam exploited the fur trade, reportedly loading ships with 1,000 pounds of pelts at a time. The river valley lay within the vague boundaries of both New England and New Netherland, but the Dutch trading post at Hartford was soon overwhelmed by English farmers on all sides. In the early 1630s, faced with land pressure from new immigrants, Plymouth Pilgrims and Massachusetts Bay Colony Puri-

tans founded new communities in Windsor, Hartford, and Wethersfield. Puritan migrations from England continued, and in 1635 Saybrook was founded at the mouth of the river.

Despite a preponderance of Massachusetts colonists, Connecticut soon asserted its independence from Plymouth and the Bay Colony (neither had assisted in the Pequot War). The dominant voice of the new settlers was the Reverend Thomas Hooker, who, after a theological falling-out with Boston divine John Cotton, led his flock out of Cambridge through the wilderness to Hartford in 1636. 🍁

The Last Halt: Stop of Hooker's Band in East Hartford Before Crossing River (study for East Hartford, Conn., Postal Office) by Alton S. Tobey, 1939. In 1635 the Rev. Thomas Hooker led a band of settlers from the Boston area to set down roots at Hartford. *National Museum of American Art, Washington D.C./Art Resource, N.Y.*

Signing of the Declaration of Independence by John Trumbull. Born in Lebanon, Conn., and trained in Europe, Trumbull was commissioned to paint several canvases for the rotunda of the U.S. Capitol. Eight smaller canvases, including this one, now reside at the Yale University Art Gallery. *Yale University Art Gallery*

Connecticut laid down its own rules of law from the start. Without benefit of royal charter, the settlers of Windsor, Hartford, and Wethersfield quickly drew up a constitution based on Thomas Hooker's reading of Scripture, which was adopted in January 1639. In pointed contrast to the Massachusetts Bay Colony, Connecticut's Fundamental Orders provided for representative government and required only the governor to be a member of the Puritan elect. The Connecticut colonists were more careful than their northern neighbors not to offend the crown. When the Stuarts reclaimed the English throne in 1660, the governor persuaded Charles II to embed the Fundamental Orders into a royal charter. The colonists held their document dear, later hiding it from the king's emissary in a hollow of the "Charter Oak."

Connecticut's legal preeminence continued after the Revolution. In 1784 jurist Tapping Reeve established the country's first law school in Litchfield. Educating dozens of future jurists, governors, senators, and congressional representatives, Reeve stressed to his students that they must defend the rights of the oppressed. He particularly championed the legal rights of married women, then considered little more than chattel under common law. 🍁

In this building, Tapping Reeve established America's first law school in Litchfield in 1784. *Photo Bernard Boutrit/Woodfin Camp & Associates*

Eminent Jurists

Tapping Reeve's students included two future vice presidents, his brother-in-law Aaron Burr and John C. Calhoun; Supreme Court justices Henry Baldwin, Ward Hunt, and Levi Woodbury, who upheld the Fugitive Slave Law while declaring slavery morally wrong; lawyers for both sides of the *Amistad* case; educational reformer Horace Mann; artist/adventurer George Catlin; geographer Sidney Morse (brother of Samuel); more than 150 members of the U.S. Congress; 15 chief justices of the state supreme court; five Connecticut governors; eight governors of other states; and six cabinet members.

Rights of All

Death of Capt. Ferrer, the Captain of the Amistad, *July, 1839. Library of Congress. Opposite: Portrait of Cinque,* leader of the successful mutiny aboard the slave ship *Amistad* in July 1839, by Nathaniel Jocelyn, c. 1840. *New Haven Colony Historical Society*

Although Connecticut passed its first antislavery law in 1784, it lagged behind most of New England, not outlawing the practice until 1848. But abolitionist fervor ran high, fanned in part by the Reverend Lyman Beecher of Litchfield, father of Henry Ward Beecher and Harriet Beecher Stowe. The issue came to a head in 1839, when the *Amistad* was towed into New London. The illegally enslaved Africans who had seized the ship were charged with murder. A Connecticut court found them innocent, but prosecutors appealed to the U.S. Supreme Court, where a law team headed by former president John Quincy Adams finally won the men their freedom. After their acquittal, the 38 survivors of the *Amistad* lived in Farmington for eight months while supporters raised funds for their return to Africa in 1841. At the time of the opening of the trial, the first citizens' petition to abolish slavery nationwide was circulated by Zephaniah Smith and her five daughters, who enlisted the signatures of 400 Glastonbury women. Local lore says that Adams presented the petition to Congress in January 1840.

Steven Spielberg's film *Amistad* (1997) was shot partly in the village of Mystic Seaport. The maritime museum's shipyard spent more than two years constructing a full-scale replica of the 80-foot schooner, due to sail the nation's waterways as Connecticut's educational ambassador.

Prudence Crandall, State Heroine

Quaker teacher Prudence Crandall precipitated a national controversy by enrolling an African-American girl in her Canterbury school in 1832. When white pupils withdrew, Crandall enrolled "young ladies and little misses of color," and the legislature passed the "Black Law" of 1833 banning instruction of nonresident blacks in private schools without town permission. Townspeople stoned the school, and Crandall was tried twice for breaking the law before charges were dropped. As times changed, in 1886 the courageous teacher was voted a pension; in 1995, she was honored as the official state heroine.

By the mid-19th century, itinerant peddlers had graduated from packs on their backs to wagons of wares.
Corbis-Bettmann

The Yankee Peddler

Connecticut commerce was built on the rock of salesmanship. In 1740 tinware makers Edward and William Pattison began to peddle their merchandise from door to door in Berlin. As their business grew, they employed an army of salesmen who carted their tinware in trunks slung across their backs on routes that stretched as far as St. Louis and New Orleans. The stocks of these Yankee peddlers, as they were known, soon expanded to include needles, pins, and buttons from the Naugatuck Valley, combs from Ivoryton, suspenders from Middletown, and Eli Terry's clocks made in Plymouth. Supplies were shipped to distant seaports to allow peddlers to restock and stay on the road. The arrival of the Connecticut Yankee peddler was a major event in rural communities, for he brought news of the outside world as well as essential goods.

The Fuller Brush Company, founded in 1906 and incorporated in Hartford in 1913, revived door-to-door sales with stunning success. By 1937 the company was selling $10 million worth of brushes per year, and the Fuller Brush man had become an icon of popular culture—like the Yankee peddler before him.

"In Kentucky, Indiana, Illinois, Missouri, and here in every dell of Arkansas and in every cabin where there is not a chair to sit on, there was sure to be a Connecticut clock."

Anonymous traveler of 1840s, in Connecticut: A Guide to Its Roads, Lore, and People, *1938*

The arrival of a Yankee peddler in remote towns of America was a singular event. *Corbis*

"THERE WERE NO HIGHLY POWERED PERSONALITIES AT ALL, NO geniuses in salesmanship or business management. Our $100 million company is the product of mediocrity since almost everyone who grew up in it was the product of failure who took his job with me in desperation, often despair."

Alfred C. Fuller, in The Inventive Yankee, *1989*

Wellspring of Industry

Connecticut began fashioning iron and brass as early as the 1660s and became a leader in machine tools by the late 1700s, as small shops responded to peddlers' calls for new wares with inventive design and fabrication. Streamside machine shops evolved into true industry when Eli Whitney invented the cotton gin in 1792, revolutionizing life in southern cotton fields and northern textile mills. Whitney later turned to the manufacture of armaments; in 1799 he won his first contract to make 10,000 muskets, even though he had never made a single one and the best armory of the day was producing only 245 per year. Whitney replaced skilled gunsmiths with less skilled laborers who could repeatedly file identical parts using jigs. Whitney's division of labor and use of interchangeable parts were radical innovations. In 1813 he teamed with pistol maker Simeon North, who carried his ideas further and introduced the assembly line.

Eli Whitney's cotton gin transformed the American textile industry. Ironically, Whitney lost money on the device, but he later made his fortune as a manufacturer of armaments.
Corbis-Bettmann

> *"No millionaire can buy more shaving comfort!"*
>
> *1934 advertisement for the Schick Dry Shaver*

Over the years, Connecticut has seen many seminal innovations: the process for vulcanizing rubber (discovered by Charles Goodyear in New Haven in 1839), the first horseless carriage (1866), the can opener (1858), even the electric razor (1931). Silly Putty, first marketed in 1949, was the result of a failed attempt to create an inexpensive substitute for rubber.

Bank On It

After the Civil War, iron banks became all the rage in America, especially after the first banks using spring mechanisms demonstrated that thrift and amusement were compatible. The J. & E. Stevens Company of Cromwell was among the leading producers of these novelty banks, showing some two dozen models in its 1870 catalogue. In one of the favorite designs, a bald eagle flapped its wings and fed a coin to its chicks. In this frog bank, when the smaller frog's feet are pressed down, the coin is flipped into the big frog's opened mouth.

The ingenious Eli Whitney revolutionized factory production with interchangeable parts and the assembly line. The artist who painted this portrait later revolutionized long-distance communication: Samuel F. B. Morse. *Yale University Art Gallery*

> *"God created men; Colonel Colt made them equal."*
>
> *Frontier saying*

English patent drawing of Samuel Colt's pocket revolver, 1835. *Connecticut State Library, Colt Collection of Firearms* *Below:* Portrait miniature of Elizabeth Colt on ivory, by Richard M. Staigg, c. 1865. *Wadsworth Atheneum, Hartford*

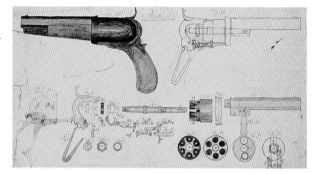

Arms and the Man

When the Texas Rangers ordered a shipment of Colt firearms to fight Mexico in 1846, self-promoter Samuel Colt opened a new armory in his native Hartford and revolutionized gun manufacturing. His brilliant chief machinist, Elisha Root, devised automatic and semiautomatic machinery that eliminated 80 percent of the handwork in making a gun, giving Colt an edge over such Connecticut competitors as Sharps and Winchester. The company's most

famous weapon was the .45 caliber "Peacemaker," favored by Billy the Kid and Wyatt Earp.

In 1855 Colt erected his grandiose "Coltsville" on Hartford's South Meadows: two armories and a housing complex for his workers. He topped the east armory with a 60-foot-wide blue onion dome—still a landmark—inspired by a visit with Czar Nicholas I of Russia. When Colt died in 1862, his widow, Elizabeth, took over operations and became Hartford's leading philanthropist. She built the Church of the Good Shepherd, with its "armorer's door" of carved sandstone pistol grips and bullet molds, and donated a 114-acre park to the city. She ultimately bequeathed the Colts' private art collection and armaments to the Wadsworth Atheneum's Colt Building.

The Faithful Colt by William Michael Harnett, 1890. *Wadsworth Atheneum, Hartford*

"There is nothing that cannot be produced by machinery."

Samuel Colt, 1854

Launching of the schooner *Jennie R. Dubois* at Mystic in 1902. *E. A. Scholfield Collection, Mystic Seaport. Below:* A whalebone and sealskin box, dating from 1825–50. *Photo Christie's Images*

Connecticut Afloat

As early as the 1640s, Connecticut River shipwrights began building sloops, sailing them downriver on spring floods, and navigating to the West Indies to sell onions and oak staves, cattle and bricks. Traces of this early trade survive in the Caribbean. For example, the old town hall of Paramaribo, Suriname, was built of Glastonbury brick. Essex became such an important shipbuilding center that in the War of 1812 the British Navy sailed up the Connecticut River to burn its privateers and merchantmen at anchor.

Thanks to its deep harbor on the Thames River, New London flourished in the 19th century, when most coastal towns switched to manufacturing. Its whaling fleet—71 ships at its height in 1846—survived until 1909. Near the end of the clipper ship era, Mystic produced modified clippers that combined increased cargo capacity with speed. In 1860 the *Andrew Jackson* sailed from New York to San Francisco in 89 days and four hours, breaking by nine hours the 1851 record set by Boston's *Flying Cloud*. The Mystic-built yachts of D. O. Richmond broke all speed records in the 1870s, until the ballast-type keel was invented. Connecticut River trade switched early to steam, with native-born steamboat inventor Samuel Morey making the first trip from New York in 1796. Steamboats began scheduled service on the river in 1823, making regular trips between Hartford and New York until 1931.

Underwriting Industry Under Sail

Connecticut's best-known corporate industry began with marine insurance, first issued in the 18th century to cover ships and cargoes sailing to the Caribbean. Fire insurance was launched in 1794, with life insurance following in the 1840s and accident coverage in the 1860s. Today the state is home to more than 100 insurance firms.

Sailing offshore of Stonington. *Wyn Drake Varney/New England Stock Photo*

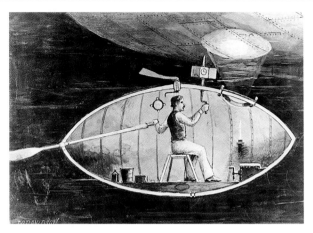

Under Sea . . .

In 1775 David Bushnell of Saybrook invented the submarine to attach mines to warships. His barrel-like *American Turtle* was just six feet high, but could hold a human operator and enough air to stay underwater 30 minutes. The *Turtle* went into battle in 1776 in New York harbor, edging up against the 50-ton frigate HMS *Eagle* but failing to attach an explosive charge to the copper-clad hull. Two weeks later it was sunk by cannon fire. But Connecticut's submarine odyssey continues. Since 1900, Electric Boat in Groton has built U.S. Navy submarines, and in 1954 it launched the USS *Nautilus,* the world's first nuclear-powered sub. Decommissioned in 1980 and named the official state ship, the *Nautilus* is permanently berthed in Groton as a public exhibit.

. . . and in the Air

Not even the sky is the limit for Connecticut inventors. Colt-trained machinists Francis A. Pratt and Amos Whitney founded the East Hartford company that ruled the early airplane engine business—pioneers like Charles Lindbergh and Robert Byrd used Pratt & Whitney engines—and continues to power jet fleets around the world. Windsor Locks–based Hamilton Standard dominates the world propeller market and has produced environmental modules—including space suits—for the U.S. space program since the Apollo days. The greatest dreamer of all, Russian-born inventor Igor Sikorsky, finally got his helicopter off the ground in Stratford in 1939. All three companies now belong to aerospace conglomerate United Technologies.

Founded by mechanics trained at the Colt factories, Pratt & Whitney has grown into one of the world's leading manufacturers of jet airplane engines. *Photo Jack McConnell. Below left:* Igor Sikorsky demonstrates one of his early helicopters. *Smithsonian Institution, Washington, D.C.*

"EVEN IN MY CHILDHOOD . . . I DREAMED about the possibility of going straight up."

Igor Sikorsky

Seed racks at Comstock, Ferre & Co. in Wethersfield, one of the country's oldest packagers of garden seeds. *Photo Phil Schermeister/Corbis*

The English settlers at Wethersfield staked their claim against the Dutch by planting crops, insisting that the land belonged to those who farmed it. As it turned out, Wethersfield's alluvial soils were some of the richest in the world, and one beloved English crop flourished beyond all experience: onions. The Wethersfield red was soon being braided and shipped to the West Indies (where it became the "Bermuda" onion). By the early 19th cen-

tury, travelers visited Wethersfield to behold with eye and nose the phenomenon of Onion Town, where 1.5 million bunches were shipped out every year.

Wethersfield soil also proved excellent for growing seed stock for most American crops. Founded in 1820, the Ferre seed company was sold in 1838 to Franklin Comstock, who added his name to America's oldest seed concern. In 1838 Franklin's son, William—exanding on an idea of the Shakers upriver at Enfield, who were selling their herb seeds in folded paper—designed brightly printed envelopes and pioneered mass marketing of garden seed packets. Comstock, Ferre & Co. no longer grows its own seed stock, but the company still uses the original border designs on its herb packets. The company's Wethersfield headquarters is a National Historic Landmark. 🍂

The Wethersfield red onion remains a staple crop in New England.
Jerry Howard/Stock Boston

"IT IS A RULE WITH [WETHERSFIELD] PARENTS TO BUY ANNUALLY A silk gown for each daughter above the age of seven until she is married. The young beauty is obliged in return to weed a patch of onions with her own hand."

Samuel Peters, History of Connecticut, *1781*

The green expanse of Bushnell Park spreads out beneath the State Capitol in Hartford.
Photo Jack McConnell
Below: Hartford's Bushnell Park was the first municipal park planned as a landscaped setting rather than a formal garden or a town green.
Corbis-Bettmann

Parks and Parkways

Connecticut has struck a graceful balance between the pleasures of civilization and the natural world. New Haven settlers in 1638 drew up the first planned city in the English colonies, with a town green whose landmarks now include the Gothic Revival Trinity Episcopal Church, the Renaissance Center Church, and the Georgian Colonial United Church. Hartford in 1854 transformed its city center from a hodgepodge of tenements and factories into 37-acre Bushnell Park, which originally contained the Charter Oak. (It now boasts a scion of the historic tree.) Road builders kept to the green theme when constructing the 38-mile Merritt Parkway in the 1930s. The southwestern Connecticut roadway sweeps through a corridor park that presents visual delights at every bend and crest.

Highway Hospitality

The coastal road between Boston and New York was heavily traveled in colonial times, which may account for Connecticut's unusual wealth of taverns and hostelries offering shelter and sustenance for man and beast. Keepers of these wayside inns often employed gifted artists to paint their signs with vivid imagery denoting hospitality. In the 19th century, wayside inns sprang up along secondary roads between farming centers such as Tolland and market towns like Hartford, where they served as drovers' stops. In this period, accomplished sign painters, such as William Rice, often dominated the trade in a fairly wide area. A remarkable number of early Connecticut trade signs have been preserved at the Connecticut Historical Society in Hartford.

Country inns sprang up all along the main turnpikes between New York and Boston. J. Carter's Inn, c. 1815, was located in Clinton, Connecticut. The Revolution marked a watershed in Connecticut sign painting. The animals and English noblemen of prewar signs were supplanted by patriotic eagles and new "celebrities," such as George Washington. *Connecticut Historical Society. Below:* The Merritt Parkway's artistic landscape design included 68 overpass bridges—no two alike—with striking Art Deco motifs in concrete by architect George Dunkelberger. *Photo Jacques Charlas/Stock Boston*

"[T]HE MERRITT PARKWAY . . . SHOWS what the highway of the future should really look like—a highway where the eye is filled with beauty and the mind with peace, as the car purrs safely along."

Bridgeport Post, *January 7, 1938*

A colorful work by Sol LeWitt greets visitors as they enter the Wadsworth Atheneum, Hartford. *Photo Jack McConnell*

Connecticut has an enviable history of bringing art to the people. America's oldest public art museum, the Wadsworth Atheneum in Hartford, was founded in 1842. Over the years its buildings multiplied, and its collection grew to more than 50,000 works—partly through the beneficence of financiers J. Pierpont and J. P. Morgan and of Elizabeth Colt. In addition to its fine general holdings, the Atheneum is noted for its Wallace Nutting Collection of Early American Furniture, Hudson River School landscapes (including paintings by Connecticut natives Frederick Edwin Church and John Frederick Kensett), and African-American art and artifacts.

In 1936–41, the Works Progress Administration sponsored one of its most ambitious mural-painting projects in Norwalk, leaving a legacy of more than 30 murals in city hall. About half are by Alexander J. Rummler and depict local farm life and the oyster industry in a vigorous, clean-lined style. Among regionalist murals of this era, the finest may be Thomas Hart Benton's series of five called *The Arts of Life in America.* (See frontispiece, page 2.) Executed for the library of the old Whitney Museum of American Art in New York, the murals were acquired by the New Britain Museum of American Art in 1953. 🍁

The murals in Norwalk's city hall, depicting local farming and oystering, were among the most extensive undertaken by the Works Progress Administration. *Photo Jack McConnell*

Ingalls Rink, sometimes called the "Yale Whale," was designed by Eero Saarinen. *Photo Michael Marsland. Yale University*

Yale's Building Legacy

Since relocating to New Haven in 1716, Yale has developed a virtual architectural park within the confines of an industrial city. The modern campus stretches more than two miles and contains nearly 300 structures, but the nucleus of Yale life remains the Old Campus, bounded by Chapel, High, Elm, and College Streets.

In 1930 the Sterling Law Buildings and Sterling Memorial Library established the Collegiate Gothic style of James Gamble Rogers as the university's signature architecture. With its soaring towers and tall, elongated windows, this much imitated style strongly suggests spiritual ties to British cathedrals and other high church buildings.

Yale has consistently commissioned buildings from master architects, creating within a few blocks an array of seminal works by 20th-century masters. Paul Rudolph created a dance of concrete and glass planes in the Art + Architecture Building (1963), where Yale's own distinguished School of Architecture is housed. Eero Saarinen's soaring Ingalls Rink (1958) was restored and augmented in 1992. The Beinecke Rare Book and Manuscript Library (1963) by Skidmore Owings & Merrill marries modernist abstraction to classical grandeur. Louis Kahn's hauntingly spare Yale Center for British Art (1977) holds the most extensive collection of British art outside the United Kingdom.

Modern Head by Roy Lichtenstein, 1974. This work stands in front of Kline Biology Tower on Yale University Campus. *Photo Michael Marsland. Yale University. Left: Lipstick* by Claes Oldenberg, 1969. Contemporary sculpture dots the Yale campus. *Photo Michael Marsland. Yale University*

P. T. Barnum and ballerina Ernestine de Faiber pose for photographer Matthew Brady at his Manhattan studio. Barnum went on to serve as mayor of Bridgeport. *National Portrait Gallery, Washington, D.C. Right:* Al Capp's "L'il Abner" comic strip was famous for lampooning the pomposity of American political life. *Culver Pictures*

In 1936 Bridgeport marked its centennial by minting a half dollar commemorating its most beloved citizen, remembered as a philanthropist and great mayor. The honoree was none other than P. T. Barnum, the promoter who had exhibited "General Tom Thumb" around the world and in 1871 organized the self-proclaimed "Greatest Show on Earth"—which became a model to armies everywhere for efficient transportation of baggage, materials, people, and animals. The flamboyant Barnum was every bit as good at serving Bridgeport, building parks, attracting industry, badgering Washington for harbor improvements, and browbeating the railroads to improve service.

No stranger to political irony, Barnum once said, "The bigger the humbug, the better people like it." New Haven–born cartoonist Al Capp would surely have agreed, using his forum of "L'il Abner" on newspaper comics pages to lampoon Senator

Jack S. Phogbound and his pal, J. Roarington Fatback. Capp's star fell just as Garry Trudeau's rose in the early 1970s. Yale-educated Connecticut resident Trudeau blurs the line between fiction and current events in his long-running strip "Doonesbury." So political is Trudeau's humor that in 1974 he was awarded the Pulitzer Prize for cartooning—the first given to a non–editorial page artist. 🍁

The P. T. Barnum Museum in Bridgeport captures the show business and political life of the city's best-loved mayor. *Photo Jack McConnell*

"YOU CAN FOOL SOME OF THE PEOPLE ALL OF THE TIME, AND ALL OF the people some of the time. But you can't fool all of the people all of the time."   *P. T. Barnum*

Winter Scene in New Haven, Connecticut by **George Henry Durrie, c. 1858.** *National Museum of American Art, Washington, D.C./Art Resource, N.Y. Below:* **Philip Johnson's famous Glass House, as photographed by Ezra Stoller.** *Photo Ezra Stoller/Esto Photographics, Inc.*

This Old (and New) House

One of the first colonies, Connecticut retains some of the earliest homes on the eastern seaboard, while boasting many exemplars of 20th-century domestic architecture. Guilford alone has more than 100 pre-1840 houses, including the oldest stone house in New England. Community co-founder Henry Whitfield built his 1639 house to serve as both his residence and a fortified haven against attack. Old Wethersfield is virtually a museum of New England house styles, with examples ranging from the 1690 Sergeant John Lattimer red clapboard colonial to ranch houses of the 1960s. Hubbard bungalows from the early 20th century cluster on several

streets in one of America's first housing developments; this distinctive two-story style features a long, sloping roof that covers a front porch running the width of the house.

Bucolic New Canaan contains more than 40 houses built by the Harvard Five in the 1940s to 1960s as "machines for living in." Models of modernism as promulgated at the Harvard Graduate School of Design under Walter Gropius, these modest homes of glass, brick, wood, cement, and steel typically feature huge windows, open floor plans, and cantilevered extensions. The most famous is Connecticut native Philip Johnson's Glass House (1949), one of eight buildings on the architect's estate now owned by the National Trust for Historic Preservation.

Even in the Federal era, Litchfield was the home of country gentry. This portrait by Ralph Earl shows the Tallmadge family in 1790: Mary Floyd Tallmadge (1763–1805) and children Henry (1787–1854) and Maria (1790–1878). *Litchfield Historical Society. Left:* Many of the oldest houses standing in New England are found in Old Wethersfield. *Photo Jack McConnell*

In Full Bloom

The cool breezes and diffuse light of Connecticut's shore and the gentle rise of the Litchfield Hills are ideal for flower gardens. Several classic gardens of the early 20th century are open to public viewing. Harkness Memorial State Park in Waterford preserves the estate gardens of Eolia, the seaside retreat of philanthropists Edward and Mary Harkness. The beds of the original 1902 gardens were redesigned in 1919 by Beatrix Farrand, who adapted British designer Gertrude Jekyll's principles to mostly American flowers. In the 1920s Jekyll created her only North American design for the 18th-century Glebe House in Woodbury in the Litchfield Hills. Finally planted in the 1980s, the Jekyll garden now blooms in its mature glory as a perennial dooryard garden perfectly scaled to the colonial dwelling.

Many Litchfield Hills residents struck a similar balance

between colonial simplicity and aristocratic aspirations. Tradition says Eliza Ferriday was inspired by an Aubusson rug to create the rose garden behind the Bellamy–Ferriday House Museum & Garden in Bethlehem. She interplanted the roses with spikes of delphinium and phlox, then drew the borders with clipped evergreens. The 150-acre Hill–Stead estate in Farmington follows a more colloquial form, with its octagonal garden (also designed by Beatrix Farrand) playing second fiddle to the sweeping "farmscape" of the grounds. The most dramatic florals are inside: a famous collection of Impressionist paintings acquired by millionaire Alfred Atmore Pope with advice from Mary Cassatt.

The Elizabeth Park Rose Garden in Hartford. *Photo Michael Giannaccio/NE Stock Photo. Left: June border at the Jekyll Garden at the Glebe House in Woodbury. Courtesy Glebe House*

Country Chic

Through her style empire, Martha Stewart has brought Westport country chic to the nation. *Photofest. Opposite left:* Nutmeg State native Glenn Close makes her home in the celebrity suburbs of southwestern Connecticut. *Photofest. Opposite right:* David Letterman may be live from New York, but he lives in Connecticut. *Photofest Opposite bottom:* Actors (and cooks) Paul Newman and Joanne Woodward reside in the Litchfield Hills. *Courtesy Newman's Own, Inc.*

Perhaps no single person has so influenced American lifestyles as Martha Stewart, who transformed rustication in Westport into an industry of decorating, entertaining, gardening, and cooking. A former model and stockbroker, Stewart moved to Connecticut when the 1973 recession hit Wall Street and began the ambitious restoration of the 1805 farmhouse seen in her *Martha Stewart Living* syndicated TV programs. A catering business led to a retail store, a magazine, and a succession of glossy books offering detailed instructions on leading a life of domestic style and hospitality rooted in the genteel ways of coastal Fairfield County.

The pastoral tranquility of rural Connecticut seems to attract people in the public eye. Television personalities Tom Brokaw, Jane Pauley, David Letterman, and

"IT WAS A MOST EXCITING DAY, THAT FEBRUARY Sunday twenty years ago, when we first saw the old property. . . . It was a Federal farmhouse, with a center hall and floorplan of four rooms over four. The proportions were lovely, but . . . it had fallen into great disrepair. . . . Here was the 'place' where we could realize our dreams of a home, and a garden."

Martha Stewart,
Martha Stewart's Gardening, *1991*

Phil Donahue live in Connecticut, as do designers Tommy Hilfiger, Bill Blass, and Oscar de la Renta. Celebrities who commute to Manhattan often choose the southwest "tail" of the state, while those with the luxury of living at a greater remove inhabit farm estates in the Litchfield Hills. The "first family" of this group is Joanne Woodward and Paul Newman, pioneers in modeling a life outside the public eye. Playwright Arthur Miller, novelists Frank McCourt and Philip Roth, and such actors as Dustin Hoffman, Liam Neeson, and Glenn Close also make their homes in the Connecticut hills.

"WHETHER I AM BETTER FOR IT OR NOT, I KNOW that notions of connectedness occur to me which never could in a city."

Arthur Miller, In the Country, *1977*

Joanne Woodward's Zucchini Bread

3 cups flour
1 tsp. baking soda
1 tsp. baking powder
1 tsp. ground cinnamon
1 tsp. salt
3 eggs
1 cup sugar
1 cup oil
1 tsp. vanilla
2 cups grated zucchini

Sift flour, baking soda, baking powder, cinnamon, and salt together. Beat eggs until foamy. Add sugar, oil, vanilla, and sifted dry ingredients a little at a time. Mixture will be thick. Add zucchini; the mixture will be gummy. Pour into two well-greased 8½" x 4½" x 2½" loaf pans and bake at 350° F for 1 hour. Check at 50 minutes; if a toothpick comes out clean, bread is done. Great served hot or cold; may be frozen.

From Newman's Own Cookbook, *1985*

Time to Sit

In the early 19th century, Connecticut clock and furniture makers put fine home accoutrements within the common reach. In 1807 Eli Terry accepted the first mass order for clocks—4,000 of them to be manufactured in just three years—and filled it using water power and the first system of interchangeable-part mass production in America. His introduction in 1815 of the shelf clock reduced clock prices from $25 to $15, and Terry's clocks were sold across the expanding country by Yankee peddlers, on an early version of the installment plan. Terry apprentice Seth Thomas opened his own clock factory in 1814; it is now the nation's longest-operating clock business.

One of the more than 3,000 timepieces in the collection of the American Clock and Watch Museum in Bristol. *Photo Jack McConnell-Right:* Connecticut clockmakers brought home timepieces within the reach of most Americans with the invention of the shelf clock. *Photo Bernard Boutrit/Woodfin Camp & Associates*

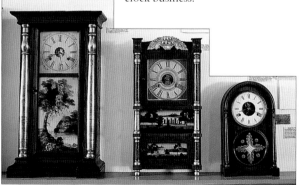

"By Industry We Thrive!"
"Rest for the Weary"

Vintage Hitchcock advertising slogans

Lambert Hitchcock took a leaf from the clockmakers' book to produce "fancy" chairs. By 1821 his Riverton factory was mass-producing Boston rockers, simple chairs with rush or wooden seats, high-backed armchairs, and all manner of children's chairs. He trained women and children in decorative painting and employed more than 100 to stencil his painted chairs with pears and plums, grapes and roses, fountains, and horns of plenty. Hitchcock chairs became instant heirlooms and luxury fixtures in hotel lobbies, theater boxes, and ice-cream parlors.

"WHY MAKE ONE OR TWO WHEN WE CAN turn them out by the hundreds, and then paint and decorate them just as clock dials and tablets are painted?"

Lambert Hitchcock

Hitchcock's painted and stenciled chairs, like this 1826–29 example, were shipped all over the country. *Collection of the Museum of American Folk Art, N.Y.*

The steel-reinforced stone walls of the Gillette Castle are finished with towers that resemble dripping candles. *Photo Jack McConnell*

Extreme Homes

Wealth married to eccentricity produced some of Connecticut's most idiosyncratic homes. Woodstock native Henry Chandler Bowen made his fortune in New York and came home each summer to show it off at Roseland Cottage, a shocking pink Gothic Revival structure where he hosted presidents and corporate magnates. The 1846 house and grounds include a boxwood parterre garden, garden house, and carriage barn with private bowling alley; all demonstrate the principles of Andrew Jackson Downing, a mid-19th-century guru of domestic design. Banker and railroad tycoon LeGrand Lockwood, one of America's first millionaires, returned to Norwalk in 1863 to build a 62-room marble "country cottage" in full-blown Second Empire style; it cost $1.2 million. His fortune lost in Wall Street's "Black Friday" of 1929, he sold the estate, now known as the Lockwood–Mathews Mansion, to New Yorker Charles O. Mathews.

The most fanciful of all Connecticut homes is Gillette Castle. After a lucrative career portraying Sherlock Holmes on the stage, native son William Gillette in 1919 built his castle on a hill above the Connecticut River in East Haddam. Gillette personally designed all 24 rooms, including one with a hidden entrance. On his death, he willed the property to the state to keep it from going to "some blithering saphead who has no conception of where he is or with what surrounded."

The pink exterior of Henry Chandler Bowen's home is unmistakable (although other architects might think it was a mistake). The estate is now known as Roseland Cottage. *SPNEA.* *Left:* Bowen designed his own private bowling alley housed inside his estate. *SPNEA*

Spinning Along

Yale students are credited with creating the game of frisbee in the 1920s by tossing around the aerodynamically shaped containers of the Frisbee Pie Company. Today Yale has two Ultimate Frisbee teams: the Ramonas (women) and Superfly (men).

Sliding By

When Dorothy Hamill of Riverside emerged as an ice-skating star of the 1970s, both Connecticut and the nation fell in love with her and with the sport. Hamill became a state heroine in 1976, surprising the experts by capturing the singles gold medal in figure skating at the Winter Olympics in Innsbruck. Today some of the world's elite skaters train in the state. One of a handful of world-class

training centers in the U.S., the International Skating Center of Connecticut in Simsbury is home to several Olympic medal winners: Canadian pairs champs Isabelle Brasseur and Lloyd Eisler, Ukrainian men's star Viktor Petrenko, and Ekaterina Gordeeva, who won gold in pairs skating with her late husband, Sergei Grinkov, and now performs solo.

Dorothy Hamill began taking skating lessons at age 8 and won her first championship at age 12. In 1974, at the age of 18, she won her first senior singles title and was silver medalist in the world singles championships. She became known for her "Hamill camel" spin. *Photofest*

The Old College Try

Lacking a major sports franchise, Nutmeg State fans give their first allegiance to college sports, cheering on University of Connecticut basketball teams, where both men and women are annual contenders for national titles. Yale University helped shape Ivy League football through the innovations of coach Walter Camp, who in the 1880s transformed the game with standardized plays, rules, and playing fields. Other sports with Yale pedigrees include crew—the 1852 race against Harvard was the first U.S. intercollegiate athletic event—and lacrosse, in which Yale first won a national championship in 1883 and was Ivy League champ in 1988–90. Yale first won the national crown in men's tennis in 1885 and boasts more wins than any other team in the history of intercollegiate polo.

Yale shaped the rules in the early years of American collegiate football, and the Yale teams were frequently Ivy League champions. *Yale University Athletic Association* Below: Photographs of Yale teams decorate the walls of Mory's pub, circa 1936. *Yale University Archives*

... *Bingo, Bingo, Bingo,*

That's the lingo,
Eli is bound to win.
There's to be a victory,
So watch the team begin!
B-B-B-Bingo, Bingo, Harvard's team cannot prevail,
Fight! Fight! Fight with all your might for Bingo,
Bingo,
Eli Yale!

Words and music by Cole Porter, class of 1913, who did his part by penning this and another fight song, "Bull-Dog"

Hartford Literati

Connecticut's contributions to American letters began with the late-18th-century "Hartford Wits"—an early literary circle, noted for political satires. Only Timothy Dwight is remembered today, mostly for his role as president of Yale. Decades later, semirural West Hartford became the site of a literary and social experiment: Nook Farm, a short-lived intellectual utopia dominated by the Beecher clan, with its causes from suffrage to free love. Its literary beacon was Harriet Beecher Stowe, author of *Uncle Tom's Cabin.*

The Connecticut Yankee

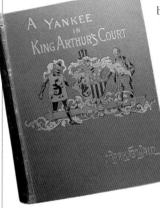

Olivia and Samuel Clemens adopted Nook Farm in 1871, building an elaborate house next door to Stowe's. Clemens chose Hartford in part because his subscription publisher, Elisha Bliss, was based there. With Olivia's inheritance and Sam's earnings as "Mark Twain," they built a mansion befitting his ascendant literary star, hiring Louis Comfort Tiffany to decorate the interiors (the only Tiffany interiors still intact). *Atlantic Monthly* editor William Dean Howells wrote, "The Clemenses are whole-souled hosts, with inextinguishable money, and a palace of a house." Despite the entertaining, Clemens managed to write furiously in his billiards room, completing *Tom Sawyer, Huckleberry Finn, The Prince and the Pauper, Life on the Mississippi,* and *A Connecticut Yankee in King Arthur's Court* before leaving the house in 1891.

Mark Twain's personal copy of *A Connecticut Yankee in King Arthur's Court.* (The word "Connecticut" does not appear until the title page.) Mark Twain House, Hartford

> ## *"The ornament of the house is the friends who frequent it."*
>
> Inscription on the library fireplace in Mark Twain House

Man of Many Words
West Hartford–born Noah Webster gave America its linguistic independence, first in multiple editions of his *American Spelling Book* issued 1776–83. In 1828 he released the revolutionary *American Dictionary of the English Language*, the bible of standard American speech and literature. (Later editions dropped "American" from the title.)

"I AM AN AMERICAN. I WAS BORN AND REARED IN HARTFORD, in the State of Connecticut—anyway, just over the river, in the country. So I am a Yankee of the Yankees— and practical, yes; and nearly barren of sentiment, I suppose—or poetry, in other words. . . . Why, I could make anything a body wanted—anything in the world, it didn't make any difference what; and if there wasn't any quick new-fangled way to make a thing, I could invent one—and do it as easy as rolling off a log."

Mark Twain, A Connecticut Yankee in King Arthur's Court, *1889*

Samuel L. Clemens—"Mark Twain"—Hartford's most flamboyant literary figure, poses with his family on the porch. From left: daughter Clara, wife Olivia, daughter Jean, Samuel, daughter Susie. The dog was named Hash. *Mark Twain Memorial, Hartford*

Eugene O'Neill won his first Pulitzer Prize for drama in 1920. *Culver Pictures*

Although born in New York, Nobel Prize laureate Eugene O'Neill grew up in New London, a place and time he remembered both fondly—in his only comedy, the nostalgic *Ah, Wilderness!*—and darkly, in the Pulitzer Prize–winning *Long Day's Journey Into Night.* His boyhood home and the setting for both plays, Monte Cristo Cottage, is a museum of O'Neill memorabilia furnished according to the stage directions for *Long Day's Journey.*

Connecticut's proximity to New York has made it an incubator for American drama and musical comedy. Since opening in 1914, New Haven's Shubert Theatre has been the scene of 600 pre-Broadway tryouts, half of them premieres. Rodgers and Hammerstein considered the Shubert their "lucky" theater after collaborating here for the first time in 1943 on *Away We Go!,* which was renamed in Boston for its new song, *Oklahoma!* They also premiered *Carousel, South Pacific,* and *The King and I* at the Shubert. Other world premieres at the old house included *A Streetcar Named Desire, My Fair Lady,* and Neil Simon's *Barefoot in the Park.*

The Goodspeed Opera House is located on the Connecticut River, near the famous Chester-Hadlyme Ferry, which has run since 1769. *Photo Jack McConnell. Below: "Racing the Clock" from The Pajama Game,* a 1998 revival at the Goodspeed Opera House in East Haddam. *Photo Diane Sobolewski. Courtesy Goodspeed Opera House*

New Haven's Long Wharf Theatre has sent more than 20 plays to Broadway, Off-Broadway, and public television, including its premieres of *The Crucible* and *Broken Glass* by Arthur Miller, who lives in Roxbury in the Litchfield Hills. The Goodspeed Opera House in East Haddam on the Connecticut River was built in 1876 in the heyday of Victorian melodrama. Since its 1959 reactivation, the Goodspeed has been dedicated to preserving and advancing musical theater, premiering such hits as *Annie, Shenandoah,* and *Man of La Mancha.*

The Eugene O'Neill Theater Center in Waterford and the Yale School of Drama develop young playwrights, train actors and directors, and foster intelligent stage criticism. The Yale Repertory Theater has premiered four plays by August Wilson as well as Athol Fugard's "Yale trilogy," which includes the hit *Master Harold and the Boys.* Among the most famous of Yale's theatrical graduates are actors Meryl Streep and Sigourney Weaver. 🍁

Death of a Salesman made the career of playwright Arthur Miller. *Photofest. Right:* The Yale Repertory Theater has been instrumental in developing the plays of August Wilson and Athol Fugard. *Photo Jack McConnell*

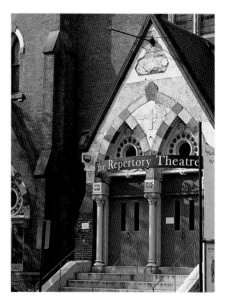

Maintaining her Connecticut Yankee accent throughout her distinguished career, Hartford's Katharine Hepburn has won four Academy Awards for her acting. *Culver Pictures*

Connecticut's Queen of the Screen

With four Academy Awards for best actress or best supporting actress and a dozen nominations, Katharine Hepburn, born in Hartford in 1906, practically defined the patrician Yankee in a stage, film, and television career that began with a bit part on Broadway in 1928. After a series of ever larger stage roles, she made the jump to Hollywood with *A Bill of Divorcement,* her first of dozens of starring roles, and won her first Oscar in 1933 for *Morning Glory.* Her other Academy Award–winning performances were in *Guess Who's Coming to Dinner* (1967), *The Lion in Winter* (1968), and *On Golden Pond* (1981).

The Charles Ives birthplace in Danbury is now a museum. *Photo Jack McConnell. Right:* Charles Ives wrote almost all his music before 1910, but little of it was performed until the 1940s. *Culver Pictures*

Variations on America

Born in 1874 in Danbury, Charles Edward Ives managed to combine practicality in business with radical experimentalism in music. Taught the basics of counterpoint and harmony by his father, George, a Civil War bandmaster and experimenter with quotidian sounds, Ives studied music at Yale but pursued an extremely successful career in insurance. Composing to satisfy his creative needs, Ives was among the first to employ polytonality, cross rhythms, and atonality in his music, most of which was not published until after he quit composing. He was awarded the Pulitzer Prize for his *Third Symphony,* written 1901–10 but first performed in 1946. He died in 1954 and was designated Connecticut's official state composer in 1991.

Ideas of Order at "The Hartford"

Wallace Stevens was 37 when he moved to Hartford from New York in 1916, an established expert in fidelity and surety insurance claims. Over the next four decades, he carved out a fiercely aesthetic approach to poetry, while keeping his day job as an insurance executive. Longtime friend of philosopher George Santayana, whom he met as a Harvard undergraduate, Stevens developed into the most insistently intellectual of American poets. In 1955, shortly before his death, he was awarded the Pulitzer Prize for his *Collected Poems* and an honorary degree by Yale, which he called "the greatest prize for a Harvard man."

Insurance executive Wallace Stevens was the definitive modern American poet. *Culver Pictures*

A MYTHOLOGY REFLECTS ITS REGION. HERE
In Connecticut, we never lived in a time
When mythology was possible—But if we had—
That raises the question of the image's truth.
The image must be of the nature of its creator.
It is the nature of its creator increased,
Heightened. It is he, anew, in a freshened youth
And it is he in the substance of his region
Wood of his forests and stone out of his fields
Or from under his mountains.

Wallace Stevens, untitled poem from Late Poems (1950–55)

Yale-educated Cole Porter was one of America's best-loved songwriters and composers.
Culver Pictures

Connecticut's Puritans frowned on music beyond the five sacred tunes to which all hymns were fitted. Not until the early 19th century did a few inspired teachers form a wide range of choral societies, choirs, and glee clubs such as Hartford's Euterpian Society. The first music school for teachers was established in 1839 by piano maker Orramel Whittesley; when two of his piano students were forced to stay the night during a blizzard, Whittesley realized he had a better future in running a boarding school for music than in building pianos. At its height, the Music Vale Seminary in Salem enrolled students from as far away as the deep South, Canada, the West Indies, and the Midwest. Musical pedagogy continues strong with conservatory training at the Hartt School in Hartford and at Yale's noted graduate school of music.

The Hartford Symphony, the state's premier professional orchestra, presents more than 60 concerts per year at the Art Deco Bushnell Memorial Hall.

Performance of *Madame Butterfly* at Bushnell Memorial Hall in 1979. *Photo Jack McConnell*

Summer programs abound. Music Mountain in Falls Village, founded in the late 1920s, is the country's oldest continuing chamber music festival. The Yale Summer School of Music has hosted the Norwalk Chamber Music Festival each year since 1941. 🦋

Tea in the Arbor by Elmer Livingston MacRae, 1911. A guest who came to paint at the Bush-Holley House in Cos Cob, MacRae fell in love with the innkeeper's daughter, married her, and lived at the inn until his death in the 1950s. *Bruce Museum, Greenwich*

New York painters dazzled by the plein-air art they saw in Paris didn't have to look beyond the Connecticut coast to find subjects for American Impressionism. In the 1880s, John Henry Twachtman and J. Alden Weir began visiting the hamlet of Cos Cob, spending weeks each summer lugging their easels around to paint the village, mill pond, and harbor. The art school they established behind the Bush-Holley boardinghouse in 1891 grew into an art colony that lasted 30 years.

In the 1890s Weir's private farmstead a few miles inland at Wilton became a retreat for painters experimenting with pure, prismatic pigments unmixed on the canvas to produce intense coloration and flickering light. Frequent visitors to Weir Farm, now a National Historic Site, included Twachtman, Childe Hassam, and Albert Pinkham Ryder, each of whom painted some of his finest landscapes here. Old Lyme was the most enduring of the Impressionist

"... GO OUT INTO THE COUNTRY AND PAINT WITH A STICK— look at nature and get the paint on anyhow."

J. Alden Weir's advice to a student

The Barns at Windham by J. Alden Weir, c. 1905. A catalytic figure in American Impressionism, Weir established a farm in the Connecticut countryside, now a National Historic Site, where many of the American Impressionists came to paint. *Adelson Galleries, New York*

colonies. On its south lay great saltwater marshes, on the north rolling meadows and oak woods. Georgian and Federal architecture dotted the village, and outlying farms were rimmed with long stone walls. Beginning in 1900, many painters boarded with Florence Griswold, whose home is now a museum, and they vied to paint the

End of Winter by John Henry Twachtman, c. 1889. Twachtman was among the first New York painters to seek inspiration in the Connecticut countryside. *National Museum of American Art, Washington, D.C./Art Resource, N.Y.*

wooden panels in the dining room. Two of the finest are by Willard Metcalf and Childe Hassam, whose bright and broken colors render the shifting, elusive character of shore light.

Many less-famous artists took up residence in Old Lyme and formed the Lyme Art Association, which painters and sculptors could join only by invitation. They built the nation's first artist-financed gallery, the Lyme Art Gallery, which opened in 1921—just as Impressionism was going out of vogue. Undaunted, the association persists, holding members' shows in the fall and spring and art sales over the summer. 🍁

"WE HAVE TENDED TO IGNORE THAT IT WAS the first and largest art colony of its kind and that many of the forward spirits in the art world during the first decades of this century either worked at Old Lyme or were closely associated with the group. . . . But most important, the art colony at Old Lyme developed a style— a way of looking at nature that was uniquely its own."

Jane Hayward, preface to catalogue
The Art Colony at Old Lyme, 1900–1935, 1966

The News Depot, Cos Cob, Connecticut by Childe Hassam, 1912. *Above: The Mill Pond, Cos Cob, Connecticut* by Childe Hassam, 1903. After studying painting in Boston and Paris, Hassam became one of the foremost American exponents of Impressionism. His work is characterized by luminous atmosphere, intense coloration, and the narrative eye of a natural voyeur. *Both, Photo Christie's Images*

Illustrator, engineer, and sculptor Alexander Calder in his studio in Roxbury. *Photo Hans Namuth/Photo Researchers*

Calder in Connecticut

Alexander Calder established his principal U.S. studio in Roxbury in 1933 shortly after beginning to make mobiles (a term coined by Marcel Duchamp) and stabiles (coined by Jean Arp) in Paris. He set up his first outdoor mobile, *Steel Fish,* in Roxbury in 1934. Although Calder was well-known in Europe for his small sculptures—especially his wire circus figures—his American breakthrough came in 1939 when the Museum of Modern Art commissioned his first large mobile, *Lobster Trap and Fish Tail,* for the main stairwell of its new West 53rd Street building. In the catalogue of a 1946 Paris exhibition, Jean-Paul Sartre described Calder's mobiles as "at once lyrical inventions, technical combinations of an almost mathematical quality, and sensitive symbols of nature."

After 1953 Calder also maintained a studio in France, but Connecticut, with its foundries and metalworking traditions, remained essential as the scale of his work grew. By 1958 Calder had three metal shops—two in Waterbury and one in Watertown—fabricating his pieces, and he commented that he felt like "a big businessman as I drove from one to another." While he loomed large on the international art scene, Calder remained quintessentially American in his pragmatism and technical ingenuity, coupled with an imagination forever at play.

A Horse of a Different Shape

In her 1906 will, Ella Burr McManus bequeathed $50,000 to create a sculptural drinking fountain for horses, specifying that the Connecticut State Capitol Commission employ "the most competent and gifted sculptor" they could find. The project bounced around for more than 50 years until the bequest had swollen to $1.2 million. When the commission finally settled on Calder, he indulged his whimsy by replacing the horse with a dinosaur, creating the monumental red stabile *Stegosaurus,* now a landmark in Burr Mall next to the Wadsworth Atheneum.

The Praying Mantis by Alexander Calder, 1936. *Wadsworth Atheneum, Hartford*

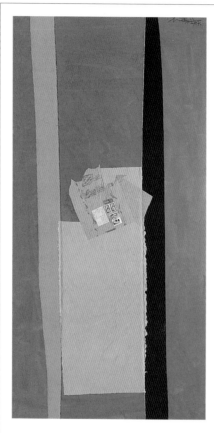

Abstraction and Conception

Two leading figures in the post-1950 art world, Robert Motherwell and Sol LeWitt, have had close ties to Connecticut. Motherwell, one of the chief spokesmen for Abstract Expressionism, infused European avant-garde intellectualism into American nonfigurative painting. Yet he insisted on the importance of thematic content, and his works had a strong political component as early as 1941. In 1949, he began painting the Rorschach-like black blots on light ground that became his signature motif. Long a fixture on the New York scene, in 1971 Motherwell moved to a restored carriage house in Greenwich with seven studios, including a SoHo-style loft, where he continued to make paintings, etchings, lithographs, and collages until his death in 1991.

Sculptor and graphic artist Sol LeWitt is a guiding light of Conceptual art, itself a reaction to Abstract Expressionism. Born in Hartford in 1928, LeWitt went to New York right after college and worked initially as a graphic designer, at one point laboring in the graphics division of the I. M. Pei architectural firm. LeWitt pared his work down to bare geometric essentials but has always rejected the "minimalist" tag. LeWitt retains a strongly amicable relationship with Hartford's Wadsworth Atheneum. His large-scale architectural installation dominates one of the entries, and the artist donated his extensive private collection of modern art to the museum.

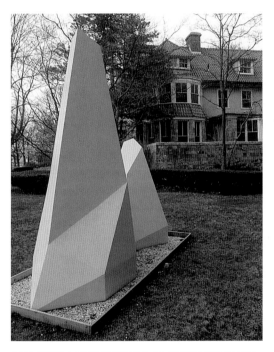

Complex Form #4 by Sol LeWitt, 1987. New Britain Museum of American Art. Opposite: The Spanish Poet (Jose de Expronceda, 1808–42) by Robert Motherwell, 1976. © Dedalus Foundation, Inc. Licensed by VAGA, New York, N.Y. Courtesy The William Benton Museum of Art

"CONCEPTUAL ART IS MADE TO ENGAGE THE MIND OF THE viewer rather than his eye or emotions."

Sol LeWitt, in Artforum, *1976*

Atlantic by Elizabeth Enders, 1992. Born in New London, Enders studied at Connecticut College before moving to New York to do graduate work at New York University and study painting at the School of Visual Arts. *Photo Zindman/Fremont. Courtesy the artist*

The dappled landscape and relentless sea that captivated the American Impressionists at the dawn of the 1900s continues to entrance painters as another century begins. The Lyme Art Association, formed in the art colony's heyday, is still active, its gallery mounting seven shows each year of painters working in the local tradition. The Lyme Academy of Fine Arts provides training for contemporary artists and runs a regular exhibition program in its gallery. The southern Connecticut coast, where New York artists first ventured, retains a lively art scene, with a concentration of galleries in Westport.

The rustic beauty and colonial milieu of the Litchfield Hills, where Alexander Calder and Yves Tanguy broke new ground decades earlier, continues to attract a diverse group of painters, working both in representational and abstract modes. The town of Kent is renowned for its outstanding art galleries, and the Kent Art Association, more than 75 years old, boasts a gallery of its own that exhibits paintings and sculptures by artists from throughout the Northeast.

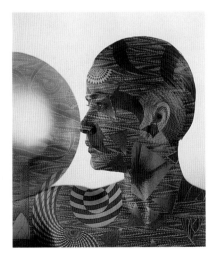

Untitled by Ellen Carey, 1987. Carey's 20x24" Polaroid print self-portraits make use of arresting patterns and colors. Edwin Land, who invented the instant photographic process and founded Polaroid Corporation, was a native of Connecticut. *Courtesy Jayne H. Baum/ JHB Gallery. Copyright Ellen Carey, 1987*

Griffon by David Hayes, 1989. Born in Hartford in 1931, David Hayes is often considered Connecticut's leading contemporary abstract sculptor. He works principally in steel and has installed a number of his sculptures on his 53-acre farm in Coventry. *Courtesy the artist*
Opposite: The Skier by Frederick L. Schavoir, 1986. Schavoir is one of many artists based in Old Lyme, a vibrant art colony for more than a century. *Courtesy the artist*

Studio programs at educational institutions continue to bring fresh blood to the Connecticut scene, with Yale's Master of Fine Arts program drawing highly talented artists in a range of media. The Hartford School of Art, now part of the University of Hartford, has a venerable tradition of training commercial and fine artists, and operates a lively gallery of changing exhibitions.

Although the Wadsworth Atheneum is the country's oldest public art museum, it is keenly attuned to the pulse of contemporary art, amassing a superb collection of 20th-century work and mounting an exemplary program of exhibitions. In contrast to the patrician Atheneum, Hartford's Real Art Ways operates three galleries for new and experimental art, video screenings, and performance art. The Whitney Museum of American Art at Champion in Stamford leavens the home-grown with changing shows that reflect New York–centered curatorial concepts. And the now-gritty industrial city of Norwalk has become a place for new art to blossom, especially in its waterfront district known affectionately as SoNo—a South Norwalk twist on Manhattan's SoHo. The area is especially noted for its three-day SoNo Arts Celebration held in August. With predictable irony, the artists have made SoNo so fashionable that they soon may be priced out of the neighborhood. ❧

A Very Secure Collection

Connecticut craftsmen invented some of the first and best locks in America, including the first cylinder lock, so it's no surprise that the Lock Museum of America in Terryville displays the largest collection of locks, keys, and ornate hardware in the U.S. More than 22,000 items trace the American lock industry.

Glamorous Greenery

Eastern Connecticut was dotted with horticultural hothouses in the Victorian period to supply the conservatories of the state's fancy homes. The sole large-scale survivor is Logee's Greenhouses, founded in 1892 in Danielson. Specializing in tropical and subtropical container plants—some 1,500 of them—Logee's selection of 400-plus varieties of begonias is the largest collection in the U.S.

One Icon, Medium Rare

Legend has it that the first hamburger sandwiches were created in a little red-brick New Haven restaurant called Louis' Lunch in 1900. The same family still makes burgers, using the same vertical grills, a century later. They can be ordered with tomato and onion, but ketchup is considered sacrilege.

I Alone Survived . . .

The *Charles W. Morgan,* berthed at Mystic Seaport, is the last wooden whaleship afloat in the U.S. Launched from New Bedford, Massachusetts, in 1841, the 133-foot *Morgan* remained an active whaling vessel until 1921, making 37 voyages ranging from nine months to five years. She cruised the Pacific, Indian, and South Atlantic Oceans, surviving storms, ice, and even one cannibal attack. Over the years, the *Morgan* brought home 54,483 barrels of oil and 152,934 pounds of whalebone.

Steam Squeeze

The first steam-powered mill in the U.S. was erected in Middletown in 1812, so it seems only appropriate that America's last remaining steam-powered apple cider mill continues to operate in Old Mystic. B. F. Clyde's Cider Mill, which has been making hard cider since 1881, is a National Mechanical Engineering landmark.

Casting Call

The Slater Memorial Museum, improbably set on the campus of a secondary school, owns the largest collection of classical casts in the country. Among the Greek, Roman, and Renaissance replicas, originally made for teaching purposes, are Venus de Milo, Socrates, Julius Caesar, King Arthur, Saint George, and figures from the Parthenon.

Great People

A selective listing of native Constitution Staters, concentrating on the arts.

John Pierpont Morgan
(1837–1913), financier, owner of railroads

Dean Acheson (1893–1971), diplomat and Pulitzer Prize–winning author

Bronson Alcott (1799–1888), philosopher, educator, and writer; father of Louisa May Alcott

Ethan Allen (1738–1789), leader of the Green Mountain Boys, Revolutionary hero

Benedict Arnold (1741–1801), Revolutionary War general and traitor

John Brown (1800–1859), abolitionist

Moses Cleveland (1754–1806), lawyer, pioneer, and surveyor; laid out Cleveland, Ohio, in 1796

Glenn Close (b. 1947), stage and screen actress

Frederick Edwin Church (1826–1900), Hudson River School landscape painter

Jonathan Edwards (1703–1758), Puritan theologian who sparked the Great Awakening

Charlotte Perkins Gilman (1860–1935), poet and suffragist

Charles Goodyear (1800–1860), inventor, discovered process of vulcanizing rubber

David Hayes (b. 1931), sculptor

Collis Potter Huntington (1821–1900), co–founder of Central Pacific Railroad

Robert K. Jarvik (b. 1946), invented first artificial heart in 1982

Philip Johnson (b. 1906), architect

John Frederick Kensett (1818–1872), Hudson River School landscape painter

Edwin Land (1909–1991), inventor of optical devices and instant photography

Robert Moses (1888–1981), city planner, New York state director of public works for 40 years

Ralph Nader (b. 1924), consumer advocate and social reformer

Frederick Law Olmsted (1822–1903), landscape architect

Adam Clayton Powell (1908–1972), pastor and member of the House of Representatives from New York

Benjamin Spock (1903–1998), physician and social reformer

Charles Lewis Tiffany (1812–1902), jeweler, co–founder Tiffany & Company

John Trumbull (1756–1843), portrait and historical painter, colonel in Revolutionary War

Eleazar Wheelock (1711–1779), founder of Dartmouth College

Emma Hart Willard (1787–1870), education reformer

. . . and Great Places

Some interesting derivations of Connecticut place names.

Berlin Named for Berlin, Prussia.

Bridgeport Named for the first drawbridge over the Pequonnock River.

Cromwell Named for one of the first river steamboats, *Oliver Cromwell*, built here in 1823.

Devil's Hopyard Legend holds that the devil frequented this area, now a state park, playing a violin as he directed witches to brew magic potions in potholes.

Fluteville Applewood flutes, produced here beginning in 1830, gave the town its name.

Harwinton Formed by combining syllables from the towns of Hartford, Windsor, and Farmington.

Lake Waramaug Named for an Indian chief.

Lebanon Named for the biblical Lebanon.

Middlebury Name identifies town's position halfway between Woodbury and Waterbury.

Middletown This town is halfway between Hartford and Saybrook.

Plymouth First settler Henry Cook, a great-grandson of one of the original Pilgrims, took the name from Plymouth, Massachusetts.

Sherman Named in honor of Roger Sherman, a signer of the Declaration of Independence.

Stafford Springs Named for Staffordshire, England, and for the mineral springs that were developed into an early-19th-century health resort.

Stonington The area's stony soil made it unfit for farming.

Terryville Named for clockmaker Eli Terry, Jr.

Thomaston Named for clockmaker Seth Thomas.

Uncasville Named for Uncas, grand sachem of the Mohegans at the time of early English settlement.

Vernon Named for Mount Vernon.

Waterbury Named for the "abundant waters" of the Naugatuck and Mad Rivers.

Wooster Mountain For Major General Wooster, first commander of the state militia, who led his men over this mountain in an attempt to intercept British troops retreating after a raid on military stores in Danbury.

Housatonic Algonquian word for "river from over the mountains."

CONNECTICUT BY THE SEASONS
A Perennial Calendar of Events and Festivals

Here is a selective listing of events that take place each year in the months noted: we suggest calling ahead to local chambers of commerce for dates and details.

February

Hartford
Connecticut Flower & Garden Show
Features garden displays, floral demonstrations, and educational seminars.

April

Hamden
Goldenbells Festival
Celebrates the forsythia bloom with concerts, nature walks, art and craft shows.

Meriden
Daffodil Festival
More than 500,000 daffodils highlight this family-oriented festival.

May

Fairfield
Dogwood Festival
Garden tours, concerts, and the blossoming of 30,000 dogwood trees usher in spring.

Lakeville
Dodge Dealers Grand Prix
Largest sports car race in North America takes place at Lime Rock Park.

Mystic
Lobsterfest
Mystic Seaport holds an old-fashioned lobster bake on the banks of the Mystic River.

June

Danbury
Greek Experience Festival
Folk dancing and food specialties highlight this cultural event.

Farmington
Farmington Antiques Weekend
Connecticut's largest antiques event; more than 500 dealers.

New Haven
International Festival of Arts & Ideas
A gathering of performing and visual artists from around the world.

West Hartford
Elizabeth Park Rose Weekend
More than 15,000 rose bushes, representing 900 varieties, are in bloom.

Winsted
Laurel Festival
Called "Laurel City" for the profusion of shrubs on the hillsides, the town provides a free map of best viewing routes.

July

Cromwell
Canon Greater Hartford Open
Top names in golf compete in this major event on the PGA tour.

Deep River
Ancient Muster
Country's oldest and largest fife-and-drums corps muster.

Groton
Annual Subfest
Boat show, carnival, and patriotic fireworks at the Naval Submarine Base.

Groton/New London
Mashantucket Pequot Thames River Fireworks
One of the nation's largest fireworks extravaganzas, synchronized to music.

Guilford
Guilford Handcrafts Exposition
Venerable fair on one of the state's nicest town greens includes more than 130 artists.

Litchfield
Open House Tour
Self-guided tour of private homes and gardens, with afternoon tea on the village green.

Mystic
Antique & Classic Boat Rendezvous
Boat parade on the Mystic River highlights this gathering of pre-1950s wooden sailboats and motorboats at Mystic Seaport.

New London
Polkabration
America's longest-running polka festival features 15 bands and daily dance lessons.

Norfolk
Norfolk Chamber Music Festival
July and August: concerts and lectures in the Music Shed of a 75-acre estate.

Waterford
Summer Music at Harkness Memorial State Park
Jazz, classical, and pop music series runs through August.

August

Brooklyn
Brooklyn Fair
Established in 1852; claims to be the oldest continuously active agricultural fair in the country.

Clinton
Bluefish Festival
Traditional bluefish dinners cap this event.

Mystic
Mystic Outdoor Art Festival
300-plus artists display their work on sidewalks of the historic downtown.

Norwalk
SoNo Arts Celebration Weekend
Outdoor celebration of visual and performing arts.

September

Bristol
Chrysanthemum Festival
House tours, an auto show, performances, and a parade greet the chrysanthemum bloom.

Durham
Durham Fair
Connecticut's largest agricultural fair.

East Norwalk
Norwalk Oyster Festival
Marks the seafaring history of Long Island Sound with vintage vessels, waterfront demonstrations, food, crafts, fireworks.

Hartford
African American Parade/Rally & Bazaar
Floats and marching bands begin at Bushnell Park.

October

Greenwich
Bruce Museum Outdoor Arts Festival
More than 65 artists from across the country.

Middletown
Head of the Connecticut Regatta
Rowing competition attracts 3,000 competitors and 600 boats.

North Haven
Woodcarving Expo
Major national carving event features 300 competitors and 60 exhibitors.

Warren
Annual Fall Festival
Antique tractor pull, bluegrass music, and lumberjack exhibition are among highlights.

Wethersfield
Old Wethersfield Fall Craft Fair
Exhibitors feature Americana.

November

Brookfield
Holiday Craft Exhibition & Sale
Restored grist mill turns gallery to display the work of 300 craftspeople.

New Haven
Celebration of American Crafts
Juried and invitational exhibition of 400-plus craftspeople from across the country.

December

Bethlehem
Christmas Town Festival
Carolers and hayrides.

Hartford
Festival of Trees
Wadsworth Atheneum is festooned with more than 200 trees, wreaths, and other ornaments.

First Night Hartford
Arts-oriented New Year's Eve celebration.

WHERE TO GO
Museums, Attractions, Gardens, and Other Arts Resources

Call for seasons and hours when open.

Museums

ALDRICH MUSEUM OF CONTEMPORARY ART
258 Main St., Ridgefield, 203-438-4519
Exhibitions are complemented by outstanding outdoor sculpture garden.

AMERICAN CLOCK & WATCH MUSEUM
100 Maple St., Bristol, 860-583-6070
Collection includes some 3,000 timepieces, many made in Connecticut.

LYMAN ALLYN ART MUSEUM
625 Williams St., New London, 860-443-2545
Collection includes works by American Impressionists.

BARNUM MUSEUM
820 Main St., Bridgeport, 203-331-9881
Exhibits and artifacts trace the life of the circus entrepreneur and mayor.

CONNECTICUT RIVER MUSEUM
67 Main St., Steamboat Dock, Essex, 860-767-8269
Exhibitions related to Connecticut River history and ecology include a replica of the early submarine Turtle.

MASHANTUCKET PEQUOT MUSEUM & RESEARCH CENTER
111 Pequot Trail, Ledyard, 860-396-6800
Exhibits and interactive displays trace the history of the tribe and its land.

NEW BRITAIN MUSEUM OF AMERICAN ART
56 Lexington St., New Britain, 860-229-0257
Murals by Thomas Hart Benton are among the highlights of the collection of American art.

PEABODY MUSEUM OF NATURAL HISTORY
170 Whitney Ave., New Haven, 203-562-4183
One of the largest natural history museums in the U.S.; features dinosaur fossils and ethnographic exhibits.

WADSWORTH ATHENEUM
600 Main St., Hartford, 860-278-2670
Extensive holdings of 50,000 works span 50 centuries; include Colt firearms and the Wallace Nutting Collection of Early American Furniture.

ELI WHITNEY MUSEUM
915 Whitney Ave., Hamden, 203-777-1833
Exhibits trace Whitney's legacy of inventions.

WHITNEY MUSEUM OF ART AT CHAMPION
1 Champion Plaza, Atlantic St. & Tresser Blvd., Stamford, 203-358-7630
Branch of New York's Whitney Museum of American Art hosts changing exhibitions of primarily 20th-century art.

YALE CENTER FOR BRITISH ART
1080 Chapel St., New Haven, 203-432-2800
Museum founded by Paul Mellon contains extensive collection of paintings, works on paper, and rare books.

YALE UNIVERSITY ART GALLERY
1111 Chapel St. at York St., New Haven, 203-432-0600
Comprehensive museum is particularly strong on American paintings and decorative arts.

Attractions

BUSH-HOLLEY HISTORIC SITE & VISITOR CENTER
39 Strickland Rd., Greenwich, 203-869-6899

Boardinghouse for first Connecticut art colony includes a studio and fine art collection.

DINOSAUR STATE PARK

400 West St., Rocky Hill, 860-529-8423

Jurassic-era dinosaur tracks, housed under a geodesic dome.

INTERNATIONAL SKATING CENTER OF CONNECTICUT

1375 Hopmeadow St., Simsbury, 860-651-5400

Visitors can observe practice sessions of Olympic skaters.

MARITIME AQUARIUM AT NORWALK

10 North Water St., Norwalk, 203-852-0700

Exhibits explore the marine life and maritime history of Long Island Sound.

MYSTIC SEAPORT

75 Greenmanville Ave., Mystic, 860-572-5315

Recreated 19th-century maritime village features the largest collections of boats and maritime photography in the world.

TAPPING REEVE HOUSE

82 South St., Litchfield, 860-567-4501

Site of America's first law school has exhibits about the school and its famous graduates.

WEIR FARM NATIONAL HISTORIC SITE

735 Nod Hill Rd., Wilton, 203-834-1896

Summer home and studio of J. Alden Weir. Walking trails mark favorite painting spots of Weir and other American Impressionists.

Homes and Gardens

BELLAMY–FERRIDAY HOUSE & GARDEN

9 Main St. N., Bethlehem, 203-266-7596

Eighteenth-century house contains family furnishings and antiques.

BUSHNELL PARK

Downtown Hartford, 860-522-6400

Park favorite is a 1914 carousel with finely detailed horses and two chariots.

PRUDENCE CRANDALL HOUSE MUSEUM

Jct. Rtes. 14 and 169, Canterbury, 860-566-3005

Home of official state heroine, who organized the first school for black women in New England.

ELIZABETH PARK ROSE GARDENS

Prospect Ave., Hartford, 860-722-6514

Peak bloom is in late June.

GILLETTE CASTLE STATE PARK

67 River Rd., East Haddam, 860-526-2336

Fanciful castle designed by actor William Gillette sits above Connecticut River.

GLEBE HOUSE MUSEUM

Hollow Rd., Woodbury, 203-263-2855

Only extant Gertrude Jekyll–designed garden in U.S. is at this 18th-century home.

FLORENCE GRISWOLD MUSEUM

96 Lyme St., Old Lyme, 860-434-5542

1817 mansion was boardinghouse for many American Impressionist artists, who painted a wall and door panels.

NATHAN HALE HOMESTEAD

2299 South St., Coventry, 860-742-6917

Home of Revolutionary War hero has original furnishings.

HARKNESS MEMORIAL STATE PARK

275 Great Neck Rd., Waterford, 860-443-5725

Beautiful Long Island setting includes the Italian-style mansion and gardens of Edward and Mary Harkness.

HILL–STEAD MUSEUM

35 Mountain Rd., Farmington

Home of Theodate Pope, Connecticut's first licensed archi-

tect, and her parents contains French Impressionist paintings and decorative art.

LOCKWOOD–MATHEWS MANSION MUSEUM

295 West Ave., Norwalk, 203-838-1434

Sixty-room Victorian mansion known for its frescoed walls and ornate woodwork.

MONTE CRISTO COTTAGE

325 Pequot Ave., New London, 860-443-0051

Boyhood home of playwright Eugene O'Neill; a National Historic Landmark.

ROSELAND COTTAGE-BOWEN HOUSE

Rte. 169, Woodstock, 860-928-4074

Gothic Revival summer home with boxwood parterre garden; a National Historic Landmark.

HARRIET BEECHER STOWE HOUSE

73 Forest St., Hartford, 860-525-9317

Author's final home was one of country's first Victorian house restorations.

MARK TWAIN HOUSE

351 Farmington Ave., Hartford, 860-493-6411

Elaborate Victorian home has the only remaining domestic interiors by Louis Comfort Tiffany.

WEBB-DEANE-STEVENS MUSEUM

211 Main St., Wethersfield, 860-529-0612

Three 18th-century houses provide a glimpse of different lifestyles.

NOAH WEBSTER HOUSE

227 S. Main St., West Hartford, 860-521-5362

Webster's birthplace, restored to show how families lived right before the Revolution.

HENRY WHITFIELD STATE MUSEUM

248 Old Whitfield St., Guilford, 203-453-2457

State's oldest house contains furnishings from the 17th to 19th centuries; has a colonial-style herb garden.

Other Resources

BEINECKE RARE BOOK LIBRARY

121 Wall St., New Haven, 203-432-2977

Yale library houses a Gutenberg Bible and original Audubon prints; features changing exhibitions.

CONNECTICUT HISTORICAL SOCIETY

1 Elizabeth St., Hartford, 860-236-5621

Artifacts and interactive exhibits trace Connecticut history; collection includes more than 40 tavern signs.

GOODSPEED OPERA HOUSE

Rte. 82, East Haddam, 860-873-8668

Historic Victorian theater is dedicated to musical theater.

LONG WHARF THEATRE

222 Sargent Dr., New Haven, 203-787-4282

One of the country's leading regional theaters, Long Wharf premiered two of Arthur Miller's major plays.

NORWALK CITY HALL

125 East Ave., Norwalk, 203-866-0202

One of the largest collections of WPA murals depicts local scenes.

REAL ART WAYS

56 Arbor St., Hartford, 860-232-1006

Experimental facility presents exhibitions, concerts, performances, and video screenings.

SHUBERT PERFORMING ARTS CENTER

247 College St., New Haven, 203-562-5666

Stage features dance, opera, cabaret as well as theater and still functions as a pre-Broadway tryout venue.

YALE REPERTORY THEATRE

Chapel and York Sts., New Haven, 203-432-1234

Theater presents contemporary interpretations of classic plays as well as premieres of new works.

CREDITS

The authors have made every effort to reach copyright holders of text and owners of illustrations, and wish to thank those individuals and institutions that permitted the reprinting of text or the reproduction of works in their collections. Any omission is unintentional and appropriate credit will be given in future editions if such copyright holders contact the publisher. Credits not listed in the captions are provided below. References are to page numbers; the designations a, b, and c indicate position of illustrations on pages.

Text

Yankee Books: Recipe for "Clamburger Special" from *Yankee Books Hometown Cooking in New England,* edited by Sandra J. Taylor. Yankee Books, 1994. Distributed by St. Martin's Press.

Contemporary Books, Inc.: Recipe for Joanne Woodward's Zucchini Bread from *Newman's Own Cookbook.* Compiled by Ursula Hotchner and Nell Newman. Chicago: Contemporary Books, Inc., 1985.

Library of America: Untitled poem by Wallace Stevens from *Collected Poetry and Prose.* Library of America, 1996.

Illustrations

ADELSON GALLERIES, N.Y.: **75** *The Barns at Windham.* Oil on panel. 24¼ x 33¼"; BRUCE MUSEUM, GREENWICH: **74** *Tea in the Arbor.* 29½ x 30". JACQUES CHARLAS/STOCK BOSTON: **45b;** CHRISTIE'S IMAGES: **1** *Jones Inn.* Oil on canvas. 21⅞ x 30⅛"; **38b; 77a** *The Mill Pond, Cos Cob, Connecticut.* Oil on panel. 26¼ x 18¼"; **77b** *The News Depot, Cos Cob, Connecticut.* Oil on panel. 5⅛ x 8¾"; COLUMBUS MUSEUM OF ART, OHIO: **22** *Beach Scene, New London.* Oil on canvas. 26 x 31⅞". Gift of Ferdinand Howald; CONNECTICUT HISTORICAL SOCIETY: **35b; 45a** *Strangers, Resort, J. Carter's Inn. Painted wood.* 22½ x 42"; CORBIS-BETTMANN: **16; 17; 26b; 33; 34; 88;** CULVER PICTURES: **31a; 65b;** ALAN L. DETRICK/PHOTO RESEARCHERS: **87a;** ELIZABETH ENDERS: **82** *Atlantic.* Oil on linen. 60¼ x 60¼"; GENERAL DYNAMICS CORPORATION: **40;** DAVID HAYES: **84** *Griffon.* Painted Steel. 27 x 16 x 31'; LITCHFIELD HISTORICAL SOCIETY: **53a** *Mary Floyd Tallmadge and Children.* Oil on canvas. 79½ x 55½"; LOGEE'S GREENHOUSES: **86b;** MARINER'S MUSEUM, NEWPORT NEWS, VA.: **18a** Lady with a Rose. Polychromed wood. 36" high; JACK MCCONNELL: **19; 23b; 79a; 86a; 87b; 89;** MUSEUM OF AMERICAN FOLK ART, N.Y.: **5** *Heart and Hand Valentine.* Cut paper, varnish, ink. 14 x 12"; **9** Yarn reel. Carved, turned, polychromed wood. 39¼ x 16 x 26⅛". Eva and Morris Feld Acquisition Fund; **59** Side chair. Painted and stenciled wood. 34¾ x 18 x 15". Gift of the Historical Society of Early American Decoration; NATIONAL GEOGRAPHIC SOCIETY IMAGE COLLECTION: **12a** Connecticut flag. Illustration by Marilyn Dye Smith; **12b** Robin and mountain laurel. Illustration by Robert Hynes; NATIONAL MUSEUM OF AMERICAN ART, WASHINGTON, D.C./ART RESOURCE, N.Y.: **8** *Connecticut Barns in Landscape.* Oil on canvas. 23⅛ x 29⅛"; **27** *The Last Halt: Stop of Hooker's Band in East Hartford Before Crossing River.* Oil on fiberboard. 26 x 44⅛"; **52a** *Winter Scene in New Haven, Connecticut.* Oil on canvas. 18 x 24"; **76** *End of Winter.* Oil on canvas. 22 x 30⅛". Gift of William T. Evans; NATIONAL PORTRAIT GALLERY, WASHINGTON, D.C.: **50a;** NEW BRITAIN MUSEUM OF AMERICAN ART: **2** *Arts of the City* (detail). Mural. © T. H. Benton and R. P. Benton Testamentary Trusts/Licensed by VAGA, New York, N.Y.; **81** *Complex Form #4;* NEW HAVEN COLONY HISTORICAL SOCIETY: **31a** *Portrait of Cinque.* Oil on canvas. 30¼ x 25½". Gift of Charles I. Purvis; COURTESY NEWMAN'S OWN, INC.: **57c;** PHOTOFEST: **57a; 57b;** PRIVATE COLLECTION: **11** *Pequot Beach, New London, Connecticut.* Oil on canvas. 12 x 16". Photo by Ted Hendrickson; FREDERICK L. SHCAVOIR: **85** *The Skier.* Bronze. 39 x 15 x 9"; SCHMIDT BINGHAM GALLERY: **21** *Drifting Snow, Grandview Farm.* Oil on panel. 11 x 18¼"; E. A. SCHOLFIELD COLLECTION, MYSTIC SEAPORT: **38a;** WADSWORTH ATHENEUM, HARTFORD: **36b** *Elizabeth Colt.* Ivory miniature. Bequest of Elizabeth H. J. Colt; **37** *The*

Faithful Colt. Oil on canvas. 22½ x 18½". The Ella Gallup
Sumner and Mary Catlin Sumner Collection Fund; **79b**
The Praying Mantis. Iron, wood. 78" high. Gift of Henry and
Walter Keney; THE WILLIAM BENTON MUSEUM OF ART: **80**
The Spanish Poet (Jose de Espronceda, 1808–42). Collage with
acrylic on primed canvas. 72 x 36". © Dedalus Foundation,
Inc. Licensed by VAGA, New York, N.Y.; YALE UNIVERSITY/
PHOTO MICHAEL MARSLAND: **48; 49a; 49b;** YALE UNIVER-
SITY ATHLETIC ASSOCIATION: **63a;** YALE UNIVERSITY
ARCHIVES: **63b;** YALE UNIVERSITY ART GALLERY: **28** *Signing
of the Declaration of Independence.* Oil on canvas. 21⅛ x 31⅛".
Trumbull Collection; **35a** Eli Whitney. Oil. 35½ x 27⅝"